Understanding the Key Elements of Advanced Photography

Learn about making the transition from an enthusiast to an expert photographer

Disclaimer

Table of Contents

A Brief Outline of the Book

This book will discuss the introduction of digital photography and how it has progressed quickly over the last few decades. It will then discuss the importance of understanding the various properties of a digital photograph. The book then presents some important techniques that are employed by expert photographers. The finer details of these techniques are explained for aspiring photographers so that they can easily learn and use these techniques too.

This book then describes the advanced use of lenses. Lenses are extremely important in capturing images that are crisp and tell amazing stories. The techniques used with different types of lenses are discussed here in order to provide information to budding photographers who can use these methods to further improve their skills.

Next, the book aims to present some post production software as well as their particular advantages. Expert photographers often use a variety of them and here, we aim to present the particular advantages offered by them.

Chapter 1: Learning about Advanced Photography

Many people believe that they know how to take the perfect picture from their digital camera. Photography can be simple in that manner. But if you want to work as a fashion photographer, you cannot simply rely on clicking your camera to capture the most exciting image. You will need to learn about the more subtle elements of photography.

When you learn about these fine elements such as the right placement of subjects as well as the intentionally playing with the focus on a picture, only then will you begin to unravel the mysteries of advanced photography. You need to give a lot of time to your photography and learn using the different available avenues, especially on the internet, to consistently improve your skills.

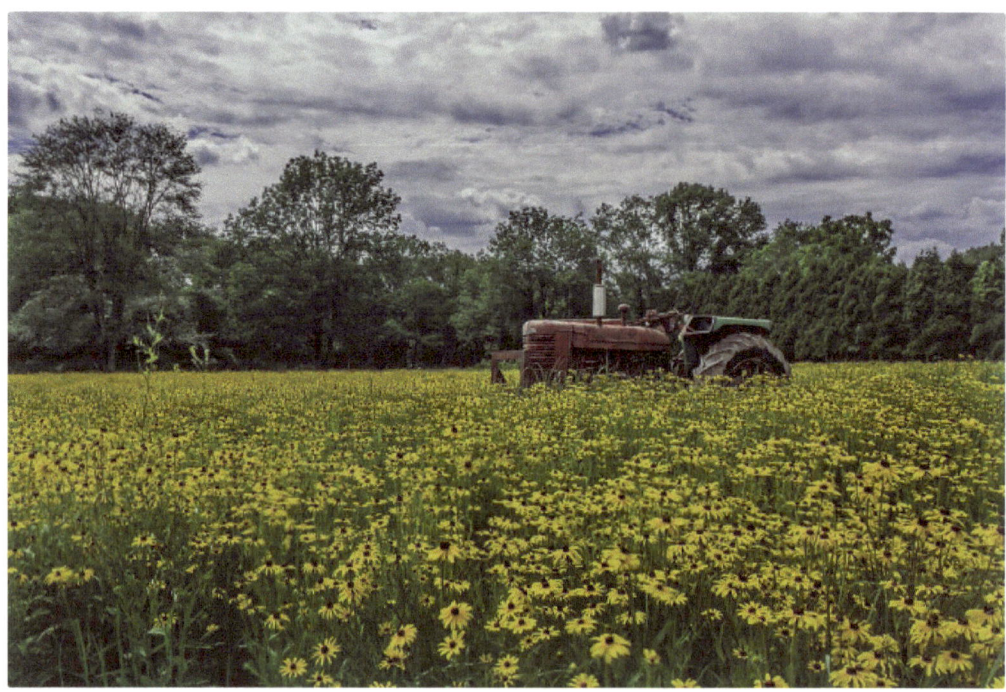

You will start to learn about the advanced elements of photography by first discovering the tools of the trade. You need to fully understand all the options that are available in a typical camera and learn to use them in the most ideal manner.

If you believe that you already know how to operate the several modes of your camera such as the variable exposure and shutter options, then it is still a good idea to once again go through these concepts. This will prepare you for the more advanced lessons.

This book will also allow you to better understand the use of RAW images as you will need to always use these images and develop them properly on an ideal post production platform. The book then presents a host of strategies that are only employed by expert photographers.

We will also share a few resources that budding photographers can ideally use in order to learn and practice the advanced elements of photography in order to turn professional and make a name for themselves in photography related industries.

Chapter 2: Understanding a Photograph

The most important thing about a photograph is that it contains a lot of visual and technical elements. Anyone can appreciate a beautiful photo, but it can be difficult to explain the reason for liking a photo over a plethora of available ones. Our own eyes perceive photos in a unique manner. We like to invoke memories and think about the impact of a photo according to our own experiences.

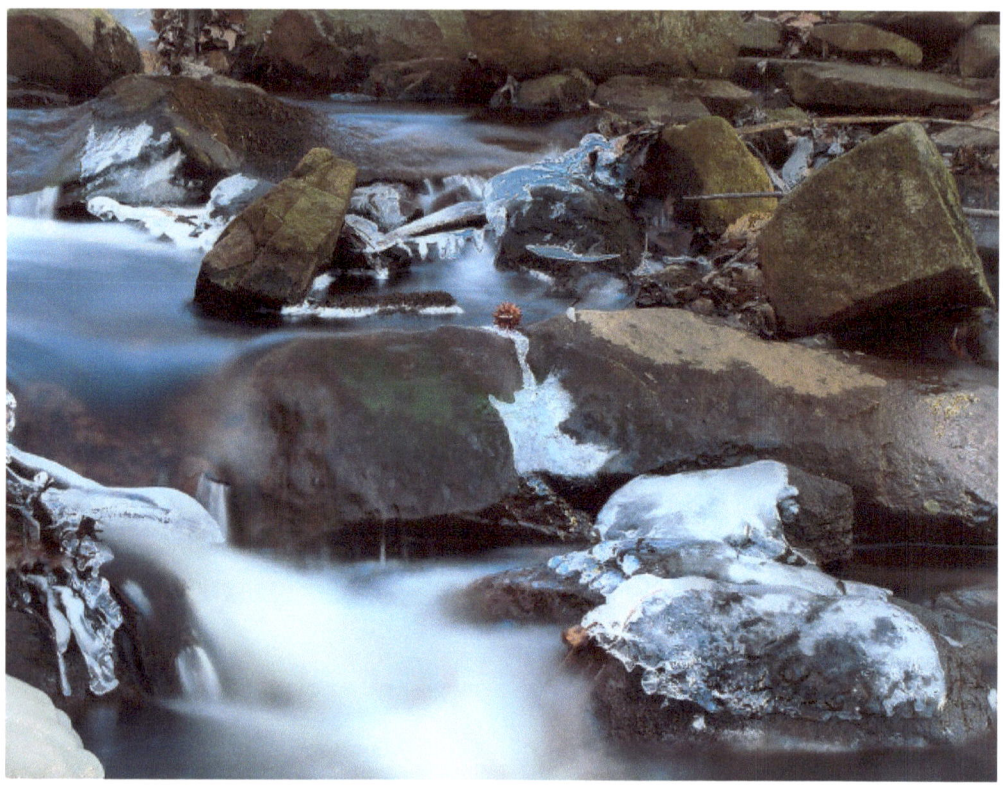

Here, we share some of the properties that you need to understand, in order to become an expert photographer.

Composition

Composition is an extremely important aspect in a photograph. In fact, many experts place it as the number one element that leads to visual pleasure. Composition refers to the way that a photograph is set up in terms of the subject and its surrounding. It depends on the way certain objects are focused in the photo as well as how the background appears in reference to these objects.

You should always try to recompose your photo from another angle if you find that it seems dull from the current one. Sometimes, a change in perspective can be the difference between a wonderful photograph and an ordinary one.

Context

Great photographers generate a relevant context in their images. Context can be created by arranging the position of the subject with the background or other elements present in the photo to tell a story. You can show the context of a lonely traveler by shooting a wide angle photograph. You can show the context of interaction by zooming in greatly on a subject performing a particular task.

Creativity

Creativity is an element that is essential for becoming a photographer in the first place. Creativity refers to looking at original ideas every time you take out your camera to shoot something. Creativity allows you to use new concepts and generate new angles even when shooting familiar subjects.

Creativity should also be used for creating your own brand. You need to find your own ideology as well as the photographer in you. You need to find a perspective that is unique and represents your style of photography.

Emotion

There will be many times where you will have to take a photograph of a person's face. Even animal faces show a range of emotions. Emotion is an important aspect of a portrait. You need to capture pictures that are able to grab the emotions. You need to ensure that your image is dynamic and tells the story of the individual present in your shot.

Your photo needs to clearly depict the mood of your subject. You need to show happiness, remorse, excitement and sorrow if you want to become a professional photographer. An interesting photo is one that ensures that the emotions of the people present in the frame are captured with perfection and can easily be understood by a random onlooker.

In fact, many expert photographers wait for the right candid moment to capture the perfect emotion, when taking pictures of famous personalities or while clicking photos at important occasions such as weddings. You should also learn to click at the right moment to capture this important element of a photo.

Layers

Layering can be difficult to implement without practice. It can be a broad concept for people to understand. The aim of using layers is to provide the viewer information which can be visualized in a number of overlapping concepts. Single layering photographs are also common in which the photograph only represents a single plain by using telescopic zoom or blurring the objects that are around the main subject.

Layers are often used by expert photographers to tell a perfect story about a particular scene by using elements in the foreground and background. Layers allow the people looking at a photograph to form a perspective. One of the important elements in advanced photography is to present important objects in a manner of layers that can illuminate important objects with perspective.

Light

Photography means to paint with light, and therefore it is the most stressing element in a picture. Light is the only tool that allows a photographer to emphasize on an object. Light as well its absence works as one of the best tools available in the world of photography.

There are different types of lighting, which can provide unique situations in photographs. There is warm light of the incandescent bulbs as well as the cool light of the fluorescent ones. You need to also watch out the impact of soft and intense light on a photograph.

Good photography is often an important factor that emanates from the use of available light. Light in fact works as a medium for a photographer who needs to ensure that they understand the difference between the daylight and the moonlight. Photographers should always wait for good or interesting lighting conditions to shoot a perspective or a random beauty shot.

Expert photographers also need to learn, that they can modify the available light. They often use additional flashes, light diffusers and other equipments for controlling the way light falls on a subject, especially in studio photography.

Timing

Timing is crucial when pressing that shutter release button. The difference between a novice and an expert photographer is evident when you see that the expert is able to wait longer and obtain that picture perfect shot. You need to always wait, especially around live subjects. If you are patient and careful, you can always get that elusive photo that you are looking for in a particular scenario.

Timing requires a camera though that contains a lens with a very quick autofocus. These lenses can be expensive, but the advantage that you gain by capturing crisp images is the one that is worth all the expense. You can only learn to time your shots, if you spend more time in your shooting environment and know every aspect of your photograph in detail.

Chapter 3: Techniques for Advanced Photography

There are a few techniques that advance photography enthusiasts must learn. These are the techniques that allow them to take amazing photos and capture what is often hidden to ordinary photographers. These advanced techniques are truly the ones that clearly separate the expert photographers from the trivial ones.

If you are interested in learning about advanced photography, then you need to pay attention to these techniques and also ensure that you practice so often that you are able to master these amazing helping tools. These techniques also help you if you are aspiring to become a professional photographer. They represent opportunities that allow you to move professionally in a number of photography related industries.

Here, we take a look at some of the top techniques that you must learn as an experienced photographer. Feel free to employ them in your photography routines to truly take advantage of them. These techniques will certainly turn you into a professionally capable photographer.

HDR Photography

HDR (High Dynamic Range) photography is a technique that has become available in the recent times. It is designed to improve the overall impact of usually a landscape photo which has contrasting parts in terms of the availability of light. It is the difference between the brightest and the darkest part present in a single frame.

Our eyes have an amazing dynamic range and are easily able to understand the subtle differences between the reflections of light that is taking place when viewing a large area.

The image that our eyes capture, are perfect in terms of the distribution and diffusion of light in a natural manner because of the dynamic nature of these images. We can easily see the diffusion and different intensities of light sources for example present in the sky at the dusk.

Cameras on the other hand have smaller dynamic sensitivity. They can either take a bright photo with high sensitivity or dark photo with reduced sensitivity. They traditionally failed to do justice to such scenes with variable amounts of light in the frame. HDR photography is the answer to that.

The camera attempts to cover a greater sensitivity range by taking a number of photos and then inter-mixing them to get a better blend of the actual lighting present in the frame. This technique is perfect for taking landscape shots at the times of dawn and dusk.

All modern cameras are built with an HDR shooting mode. It is essential though to learn to use this mode. First of all, as it involves the taking of multiple pictures to improve the landscape, it cannot be used to take the photo of a moving object.

HDR shooting provides better results, if the camera is placed on a stable platform and used to take the photo of a scene that is not changing quickly in a dynamic manner. This means that the technique is limited to landscape photography.

This does not mean that HDR photography is not important. It can be extremely important for nature photographers. You need to learn to use the mode by tampering with the available settings. Unfortunately, the automatic HDR mode on a camera does not offer the same advantages as offered by the other automatic options present on high end cameras.

Expert photographers learn to improve their HDR shooting by changing the exposure as well as using a stable platform. Other skills that you require for HDR shooting are to understand the effects of changing ISO settings on your camera as well as looking at the time of exposure. HDR photography also requires interested individuals to learn about the different Photoshop options that are available for improving the contrast difference present in the final frame.

You should also learn more about the AEB (Auto Exposure Bracketing) mode on your DSLR camera. This mode allows you to take multiple photographs at different exposures. You can then use different image processing software tools out there to perform a merger in order to create a picture. You can play around with the available pictures to ensure that you are able to finalize an image which perfectly represents the actual scene that you observed.

Another important concept of HDR shooting is that you simply cannot rely on your hand. You need to get a tripod in order to shoot the perfect HDR photos. Avoid scenes or situations where you find moving objects because they will appear as a ghost in the final processed image. This happens because the software tries to prepare an image by giving importance to all the elements and objects present in a set of images.

The Perfect Shot
In HDR shooting, there is no single shot, but your DSLR camera will always have quite a lot of advanced settings to use when performing HDR photography. It is often best to use a fixed aperture value and allow the camera to select the appropriate shutter speeds for the different shots. You can use manual setting, but then you will have to set the shutter speed as well, making it difficult to obtain the best results.

High Contrast Shooting
Another technique that can essentially be used to correlate with HDR shooting is that of employing high contrast. Sometimes, you can use the differences in the contrast to your advantage and ensure they are perfectly used. High contrast often translates into more genuine photos that are able to add perspective to the objects that are your focus of attention in a typical picture.

You need to ensure that you use the element of light in this type of shooting. You can either take the point of view of objects in light or their shadows in high contrast shooting. Silhouettes are your friends in this style and it is perfect when you are shooting hills or other natural phenomenon such as a desert floor.

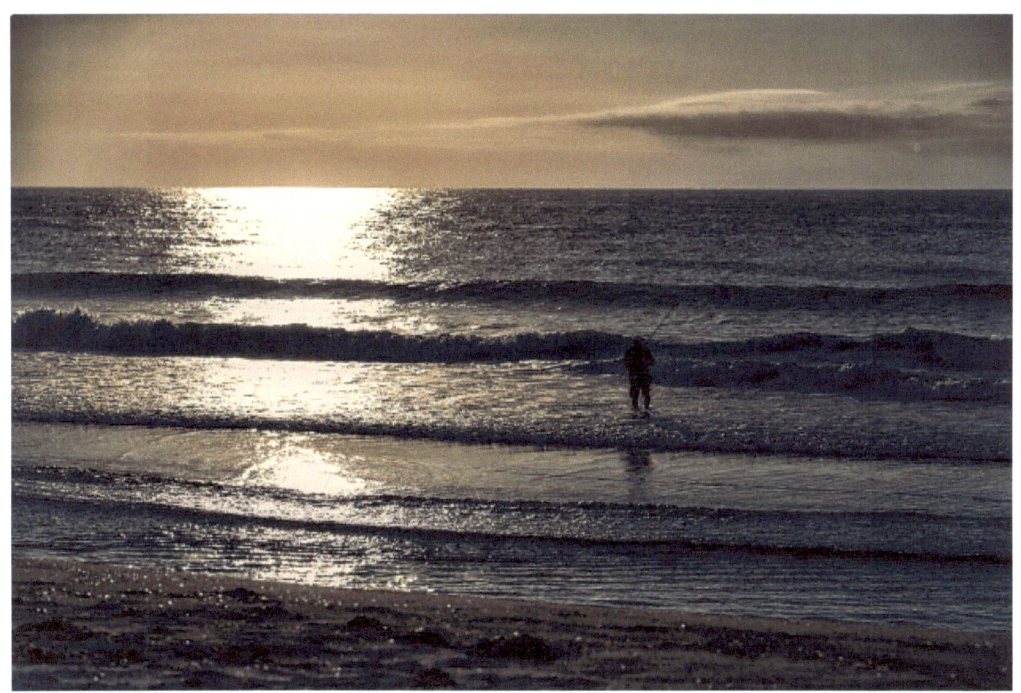

Creativity is the name of the game, when trying to play with the high contrast photography method. You need to compose these shots very carefully, because wrong composition results in one part of the shot in focus while the other portions get either completely illuminated or dark. The method though surely is one of the ways to show that you have the expertise to show a traditional scene with a different perspective.

High contrast photography is often used in contrast with the HDR photography and therefore the basic principles become opposite to one another. HDR photography is all about blending the environment while high contrast photography is all about pointing to a particular subject in a strong yet supportive manner.

High contrast photography skills are developed if you consistently practice in murky lighting conditions. Such conditions often increase the glare of the light sources present in the shot and therefore allow more room for a photographer to carefully place the object in the picture.

This photography needs to be done on the manual setting. You need to select a low ISO rating and then keep changing the aperture as well as the shutter speed to get the kind of shot that you actually desire. Remember, you can only learn high contrast photography if you actually go to different places and practice with your DSLR regularly.

You should also use silhouetting as your main way of distinctively using different objects because they will provide you a solid outline for your shot. You need to always take shots at different exposures in order to ensure that you end up with a variety of shots. You may find that your first shot was the best, but often you will find that your best shot will occur, after you take three or four shots, while making minor exposure adjustments.

Another thing in high contrast photography is to understand your depth of field and work accordingly. Always try to start with one end on the settings and then gradually move through the available options to get the best shot using this technique.

The Perfect Shot
The perfect shot in high contrast photography will require you to take a few photos using exposure bracketing in order to find the sweet spot. When shooting manually, it is ideal to use a 1-5 second shutter speed with ISO 200 sensitivity. The aperture ideally needs to be kept around f/8 to f/12. You should always play around with these settings to create your perfect shot.

Long Exposure Photography
Long exposure photography is an essential element of advanced photography that you must learn if you want to improve as a professional or even as an amateur. There are some scenarios where point and shoot technique simply fails and therefore, you will never be able to take the perfect picture of the night sky with your compact camera.

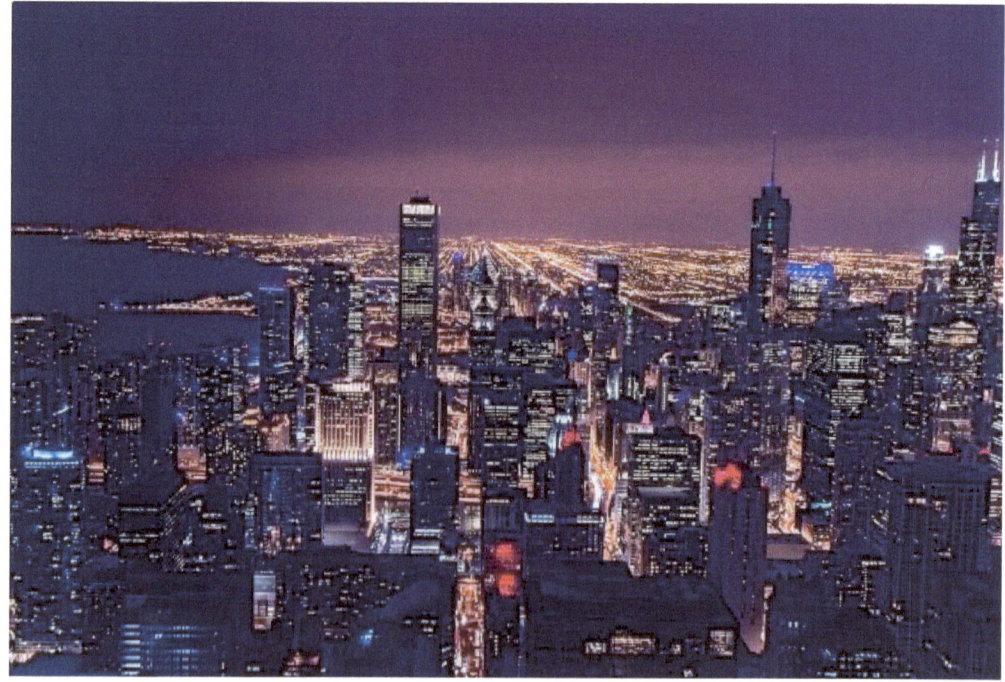

There are situations where the only solution to take stunning photographs is presented by long exposure photography. We are not talking about those 1 second shots either. These are the shots that will require patience, a tripod and an open area.

Imagine the hustle of a city at late evening! This is a scene that simply cannot be recorded in the normal manner because it would not be able to show the movements and the flickering of the lights. A video on the other hand will not have the artistry that shows a command of the photographer over the difficult elements of the night shooting environment. You require a long exposure shot that has a length of several minutes.

Some photographers are so keen on these shots that they are willing to take photos that are taken by exposing the camera for an hour or more time. You will require a DSLR for this though, with exceptional running battery time as well as the placement in an area which is left undisturbed for that period. You will find amazing photos.

You need to give this technique a try if you are especially interested in shooting at night. It gives an amazing perspective of city life and can also create beautiful rings of light when the sky is shot using this technique. You will often have to find the way to take a long expose shot in your camera. This technique requires you to work completely in the manual mode for best results.

You can change all the options in the manual mode and you have to select the camera shutter which is generally presented as an S. Expert photographers also know the amount of time to give to different settings and we are also sharing here, based on the experiences of a few experts.

Exposure Time

Water based shots can be greatly improved with exposures of a few seconds. You will be able to get a good shot because water moves relatively slowly and in a fixed pattern, allowing for an excellent photo with an exposure of 1 second to 5 seconds.

If you want to shoot a street filled with moving cars, then you need to extend the exposure time to around 30 seconds. You should find a good vantage point though, which allows you to place the movements across your frame. This will ensure that your long exposures will result in more defined objects and lighting effects.

You should always implement a neutral density filter with your lens, if you plan to take a long exposure photo in the day time to control the amount of the available light to a manageable level. Otherwise, all you will see is white in the photo with everything illuminated with no objects in true focus. It is also wise to not increase the aperture size though, because larger aperture sizes ruin the picture with degraded sharpness.

Shutter Release

You need to use a shutter release device because you cannot expect to press the shutter release button for 30 minutes. You may even find it hard to do it for 30 seconds. A remote release cable works ideally in this manner and you need to spend part of your resources to get a release mechanism. This will help you in taking the best long exposure photos.

The Perfect Shot

A perfect shot will be composed of a long shutter time of 30 seconds or more. This will be backed up by using a 2 stop ND filter if shooting in strong daylight. ISO 100 setting will be ideal with f/10 the aperture for most long exposure shots. A longer shutter time should be matched with a smaller aperture as well as increased stops on the filter.

Shooting Fireworks

It is often difficult for novice photographers to shoot fireworks. They commonly make the mistake of either composing the shot with no light or fail to control the high light which is given off by the fireworks.

The best way to shoot a fireworks display is to always use a low ISO setting of either 100 or 200. Always use a tripod for shooting fireworks because you will be using slower shutter speeds. It is better to shoot fireworks with some background such as tall buildings to give a perspective. The ideal exposure should be at f/10 or f/11. You should shoot it with a long shutter time of at least 5 seconds. Also, place the focus of the lens at infinity for the best shots.

With the above method, you will get beautiful images in which the fireworks will be presented in the form of long drawn out ribbons that will follow the complete path of separate fireworks.

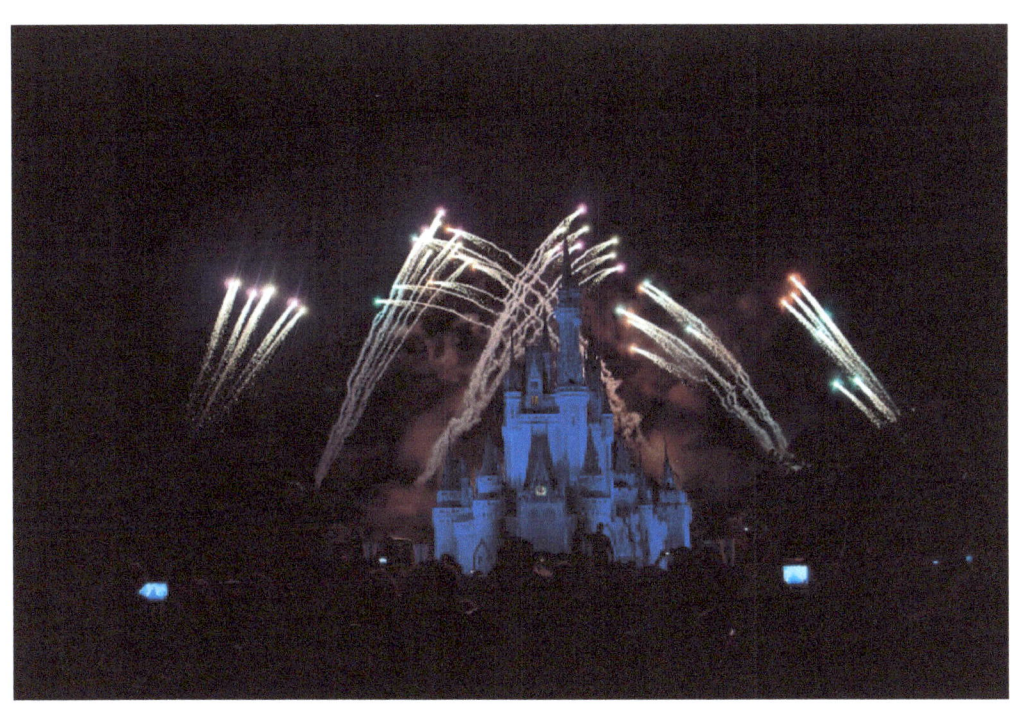

Shooting Waterfalls and Rivers

Another difficult subject can be waterfalls and fast flowing rivers. You may have found that your images look like frozen water, and do not capture the visual beauty of these natural water bodies. Here, we show you the technique which is used by elite photographers.

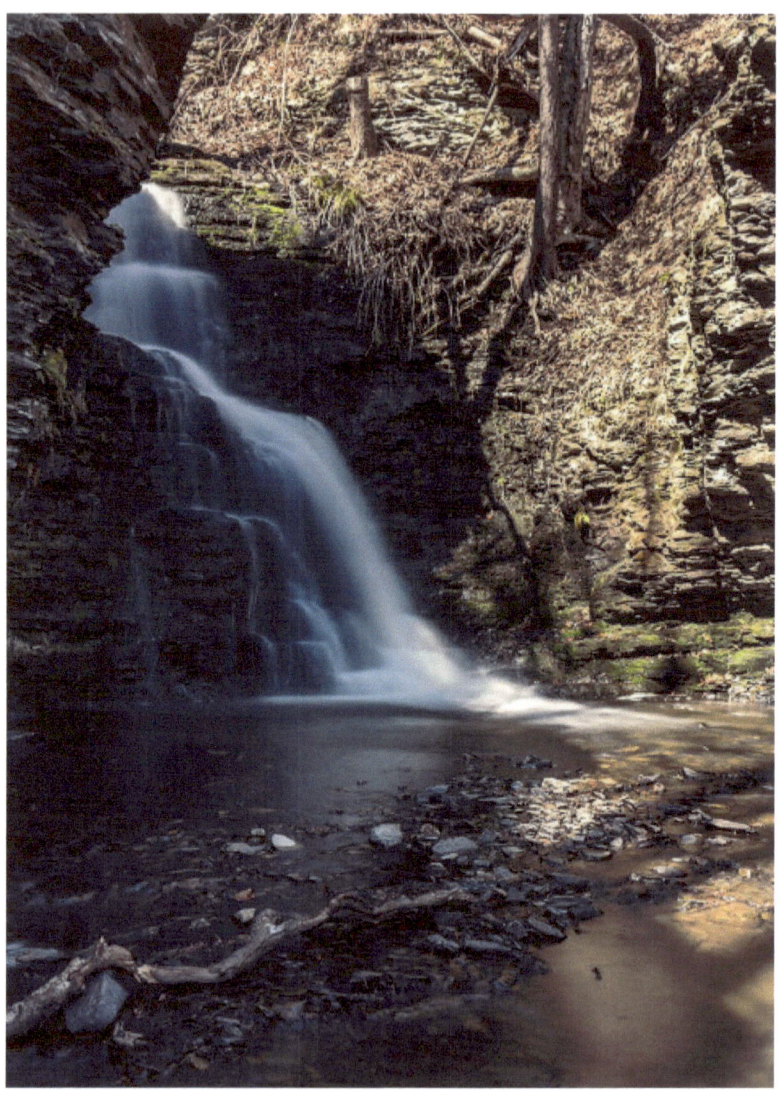

You need to use a long exposure, but this can ruin the photo in the day. A 30 second exposure is perfect for shooting waterfalls. You will need to use the lowest possible ISO setting of 100 or less if available. A 10 ND filter will ensure that the available light is reduced enough to produce the best exposure with a 30 second shutter time. A small aperture of f/16 is perfect for bringing the best results. It is often best to also use a polarizing filter to reduce the glare from the nearby objects.

Chapter 4: How to Use the Different Lenses

Lenses are the most important element in your camera, if you are looking to compose various types of photographs. You may already be family with the typical lenses that are available and commonly sold with DSLR cameras. You may own a few of them, but we find that it is important for an expert photographer to learn the finer details of the lenses available.

The knowledge of these details allows expert photographers to make the best use of their available equipment. This is often the reason that we find that some photographers can take better pictures with any camera while we cannot match their quality even with the most expensive of DSLRs as amateur shooters.

Here, we describe the advanced use of the lenses according to their types. We will start with the wide lenses and then move towards the telescopic range.

Using Wide Angle Lenses

We all know about wide angle lenses. They are able to record a picture that has a depth wider than the one we can perceive with our own eyes. These days, wide angle lenses are in common use, especially when shooting landscape pictures. They are perfect for taking shots of natural phenomenon.

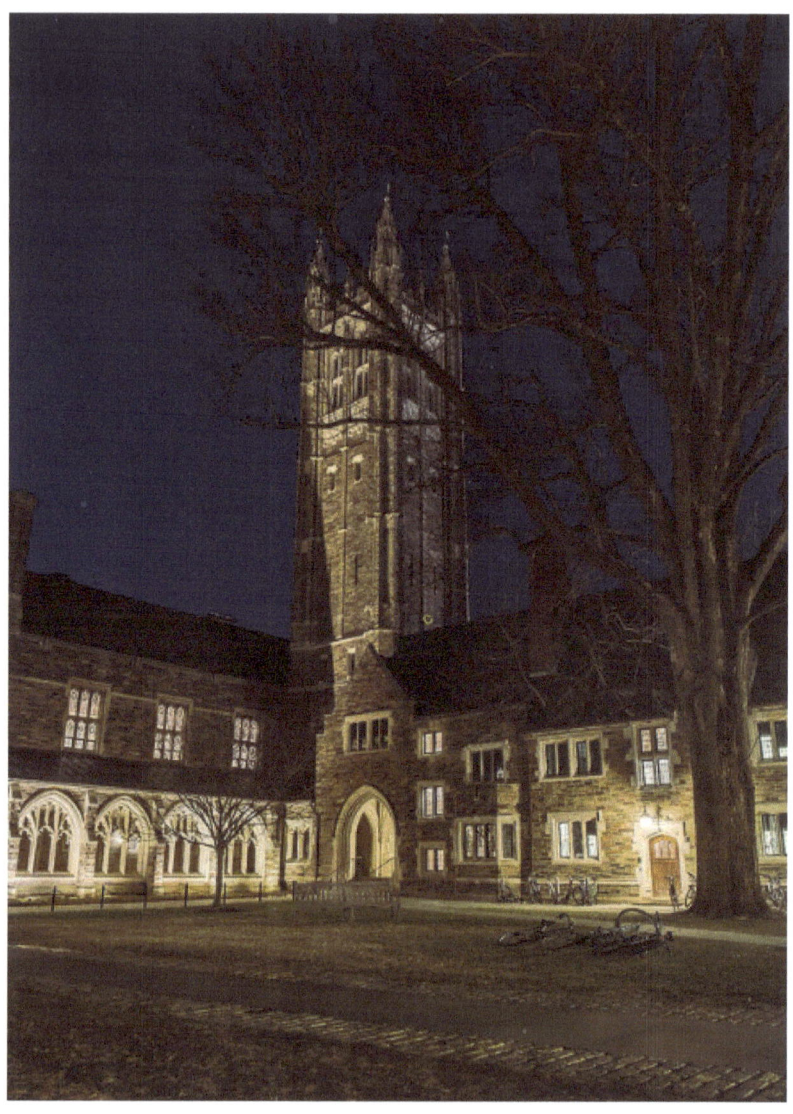

Wide angle lenses are identified as lenses that produce 35mm equivalent focal lengths of less than 35mm. Most wide angle lenses can now even go to as low as 24mm or lower in focal length, allowing them to have an extremely great depth of field.

The point here is to learn that wide angle lenses are often wrongly used by amateurs. You should understand that there needs to be a reason for you to shoot a scene with a wide angle lens. It is perfect for use, when you want to create a better understanding of the surroundings around your subject. Here are a few expert ways of taking advantage of the capabilities of wide angle lenses.

Differentiating Your Object of Focus

One of the best ways to employ a wide angle lens is to ensure that your object of focus is displayed with greater prominence. A wide angle lens increases the difference in the sizes of the various objects present in the photo. This is usually ensured, because you actually need to go closer to your subject when using the wide angle lens.

A wide angle lens also decreases the impact of objects that are behind the subject. They become usually smaller and less significant when compared to your main subject present in the foreground. You need to understand that this is the strength of the wide angle lens and you should learn to exploit that by going closer to your subjects and shooting photos that put the subjects in a strong way with the background working as a supporting plain for them.

Indoor Use

Wide angle lens can be perfectly employed indoors. You can create a great perspective of depth by using wide angle lenses to capture the images of staircases as well shooting a table full of food. The great changes in sizes are available with this lens without moving farther from the scene which is impossible when shooting indoors.

Using Filters

The use of filters can add more power to a wide angle lens. Expert photographers employ filters with these lenses and take amazing photographers. Polarizing filters can be used to include different light effects in a photograph. Because the wide angle lens takes in more of the environment, the natural lighting is attenuated differentially by a filter. This can be a nuisance for some, but good photographers use the effect to take creative photos.

GND (Graduated Neutral Density) filters are the ones that you should employ when shooting dawn and dusk time photos using wide angle lenses. These lenses are perfect for ensuring that the high contrast effects are removed from the picture and it just perfectly balances the highs and lows of light present in the frame. You will be amazed to find the results as the lighting of your dark areas will significantly improve still showing the perspective from the dying or rising sun.

There are also special filters that produce the fisheye effect. They are often used with ultra wide lenses that are able to take a very high angle picture. You need to learn to shoot fisheye photos as well, because they can show that you have mastered the best of your camera. You will need to compose your shot in a careful manner by using a variety of layers.

You can improve the use of filters by ensuring that your object in focus is best treated through the elements of the filter, while the background can be left untreated producing beautiful effects in a single photograph. This kind of photography is often difficult to find, but describes the best use of talent as well as skill on the part of a photographer.

Shooting Horizontally

Expert photographers always take of this fact because it can ruin the complete photo. Because wide angle lenses portray virtual horizon lines, it is important to understand that your object will either tilt forward or backward if the camera is not level with the horizon.

You can also use this effect to your advantage as well and create stunning photographs with amazing perceptions. You can intentionally make objects look taller or bent by tilting the camera slightly. This way, you will produce stunning results that will work perfectly for you in taking creative photos of architectural objects as well as performing nature photography.

Using Telephoto Lenses

Telephoto lenses are those with focal lengths that are greater than 50mm. Typically, they are available as zoom lenses with variable focal lengths. Expert photographers are able to use them in a variety of ways. You may feel that a telephoto lens is only there to provide the function of taking photographs of distant objects, but there is so much to these lenses.

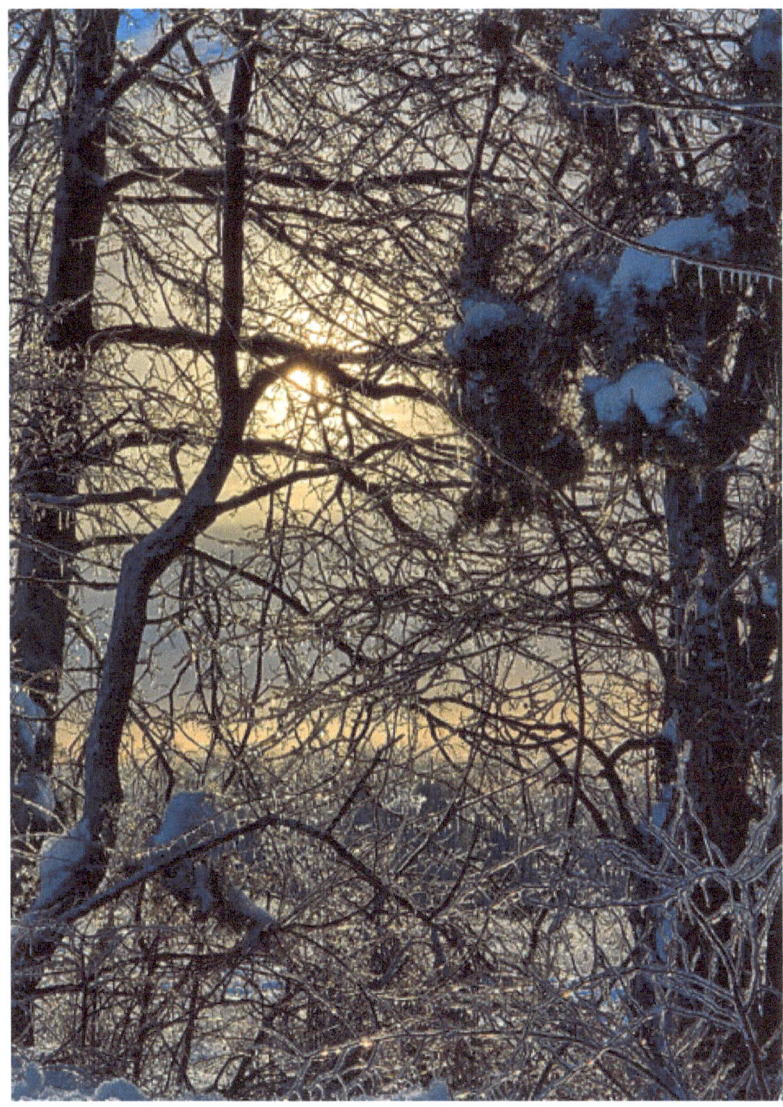

Here, we aim to present some advanced ways of using telephoto lenses to improve your skills as a photographer and get amazing photos.

Better Attention to Subject

An expert photographer should use a telephoto lens to put more emphasis on the subject. You can also achieve this feat by putting your subject as a complete layer in the foreground of the picture by using a magnified image. The magnified image should be composed to give exposure to the different elements of your object.

An example can be presented in fashion photography which is often performed indoors. You can still use a telephoto lens to zoom on the hand of a model to shoot a particular watch in the foreground. The opportunities with this technique are countless and you may find that it works for you in a number of scenarios.

Using the Flattening Effect

A telephoto lens simply magnifies part of the horizon which creates a flattening effect on the photo. The perception of depth is significantly altered, when using a telephoto lens. Instead of thinking about it as a nuisance, expert photographers take advantage of this effect.

You should also learn to use this flatness of the frame to take creative photos, especially when performing outdoor photography. Different terrain features such as hills and streams can be presented in an altered reality, if you are able to carefully compose them in your photo.

You can use the flattening effect by simply putting a variety of objects in your focus when taking a shot with the telephoto lens. This way, the distance will be reduced between the objects and they will appear as too close to each other, creating a wonderful texture in your photos.

Capturing the Weather

The telephoto lens has a great reach and you can always employ it to take some amazing pictures of weather elements such as distant clouds. Use high telephoto focal lengths to capture weather elements. An ideal way to take these photos is to ensure that you have set a low aperture value as well as fast shutter speed. You will often have to compensate for the reduced exposure by increasing the ISO sensitivity on the camera.

This technique is perfect for taking landscapes. These landscapes often have a different intensity of light and this needs to be compensated using a neutral density filter. The use of the filter ensures that colors are spread better across the picture and you are able to capture the weather in the same manner as you are actually observing it from your own eyes.

Capturing the Orderly Effects

Telephoto lenses allow you to find order in seemingly abstract landscapes. You need to look at different objects especially trees and hilltops to find a pattern. If you are patient and able to carefully study your environment, you will be able to find a number of opportunities to shoot with your telephoto lens.

A telephoto lens is ideal for exaggerating even the most minor of orders in objects and presents them perfectly in a landscape photo. You should look to find these pictures by looking at trees, rivers and also when shooting wildlife. A careful selection of a group of bucks can create the most beautiful picture.

Using a Macro Lens

Macro photography refers to a special case where the subjects have a size of around 1/10 to their original size in the final photo. A macro lens allows the subjects to have this size in the picture and therefore, is used for close-up photography. Macro photography is available these days in almost all the cameras, but compact cameras cannot match the details that are captured with a DSLR camera.

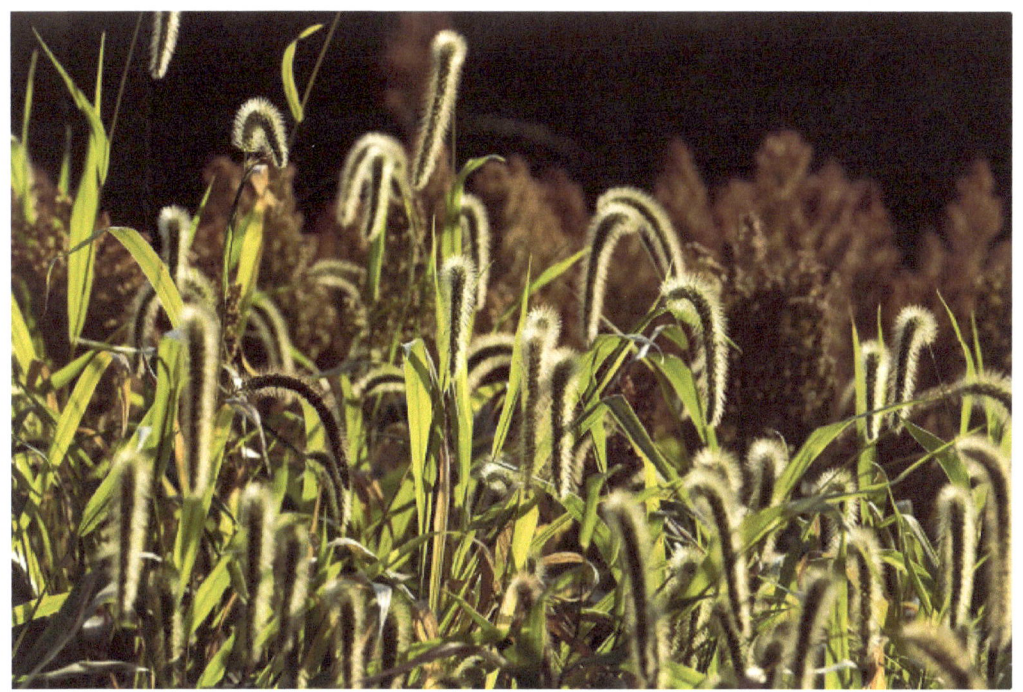

Macro lenses are available from all major manufacturers and range from 50mm to 105mm in their focal lengths. Most people buy a lens of around 50-55mm for performing macro photography. You should never compromise on such a lens if you want to become an expert photographer.

These lenses with lower focal lengths are limited in use. You have to go very close to the subjects, in order to properly shoot them with a 1:1 magnification. A 100mm lens is ideal for shooting macro photos. This lens can be combined with good exposures taken with an increased ISO sensitivity but a faster shutter speed. You will be able to maintain a foot of distance between you and the object. This will allow you to better illuminate your target without using a close-in flash.

There are also special opportunities for macro shooting. They are perfect for shooting food items and can also be used to take the photos of small insects and flowers.

Taking Amazing Food Photos

Amazing food photos is all about setting up the shot in the most ideal manner. An expert photographer is the one, who is properly arranging the light to illuminate the subject in an even tone. The best way to take photos of food items is to only use a single source of light. This needs to be a diffused source, such as natural light coming from a window or an overhead electric light for maximum diffusion.

It is ideal to use a softbox which is set at quarter power, for creating a natural and a diffused source of light. With a macro lens of 100-105mm, you will be able to take an ideal picture by using a tripod stand

and taking the picture from the top. You can use f/2.8 or f/1.8 for creating softer and diffusing backgrounds.

It is ideal to control the depth of field as well. Small items need to be shot with narrow depth of field while a plate full of muffins needs a wider depth in order to fully present the subject.

One of the items that is difficult to shoot is an ice-cream, because it melts so quickly. This can be avoided by putting the ice-cream with some concealed dry ice that will stop it from melting. You can then compose a better shot by using exposure bracketing and taking a variety of shots.

However, it is better to compose a manual shot with medium exposure. The location should be perfect and the photographer should always avoid the use of software to remove mistakes. Instead, it is better to experiment and learn to shoot clean photos the first time around.

Shooting Small Flora and Fauna

Insects and flowers present an ideal subject for shooting macro photos. They show great detail with the right shot, and are certainly a niche which requires great understanding of photography. The best way to take the shot would be to use f/8 aperture at ISO 200 sensitivity.

The photo should ideally be shot in the aperture priority mode for the best results. The shutter speed should be moderate around 1/100 to 1/250 sec. These settings are ideal for a lens of around 100mm focal length. You will need to change the exposure around the match the same quality of results with a different lens. A smaller lens will require increases ISO sensitivity. You can use a faster shutter speed with a low focal length lens to compensate for the increased ISO setting.

Chapter 5: Using the Lens Filters

Lens filters are not ideal unless used in an indiscriminate fashion. However, they serve important functions. They allow photographers to control difficult environments and ensure that they can create a better perspective. They can allow you to capture amazing photos, especially when performing landscape photography.

Here, we explain the best way to use some of the common lens filters available.

Polarizing Filters

There are times when you have to shoot in very bright conditions in the daytime. The glare and strong reflections from the surrounding objects can ruin the photo. What you need to do in this case is smartly use polarizing filters. These filters usually are circular and able to keep your central object safe from poor contrasts.

A polarizing filter should be used when taking landscapes in bright sunshine by using a slightly longer exposure yet reduced ISO sensitivity.

Neutral Density Filters

Neutral density filters become necessary when you want to take pictures of moving subjects. The ND filter reduces the amount of light entering the lens, therefore allowing the use of slower shutter speeds of around 1 second.

You need to use the ND filter when looking to shoot a waterfall or people moving through a station. You should also use an ND filter when requiring a large aperture, which is often required when using a powerful flash.

Graduated Neutral Density Filters

The best use of GND filters is when you are shooting high contrast situations as we have discussed in the previous sections. These filters are rectangular though and therefore, only used to shoot flat horizons. There are soft GND filters as well, which allow the shooting of horizon from a variety of angles. There is also a reverse GDN filter used for shooting against the sun. It works in a reverse fashion with the center in the dark.

You need to always have a GND filter with you when shooting in conditions where the sun is going down. They are perfect for reducing the contrast differences and do not require a lot of training. Just ensure that your subject is in the center of the filter, and you will be able to get the most amazing shots.

UV Filters

UV filters are perfect for use, when you are taking the shots in dusty and moist conditions. They save your lens from wear and tear. They however, do not stop the light from reaching your lens and in fact, also protect the image from the effects of a UV glare.

Chapter 6: Top Post Production Tools

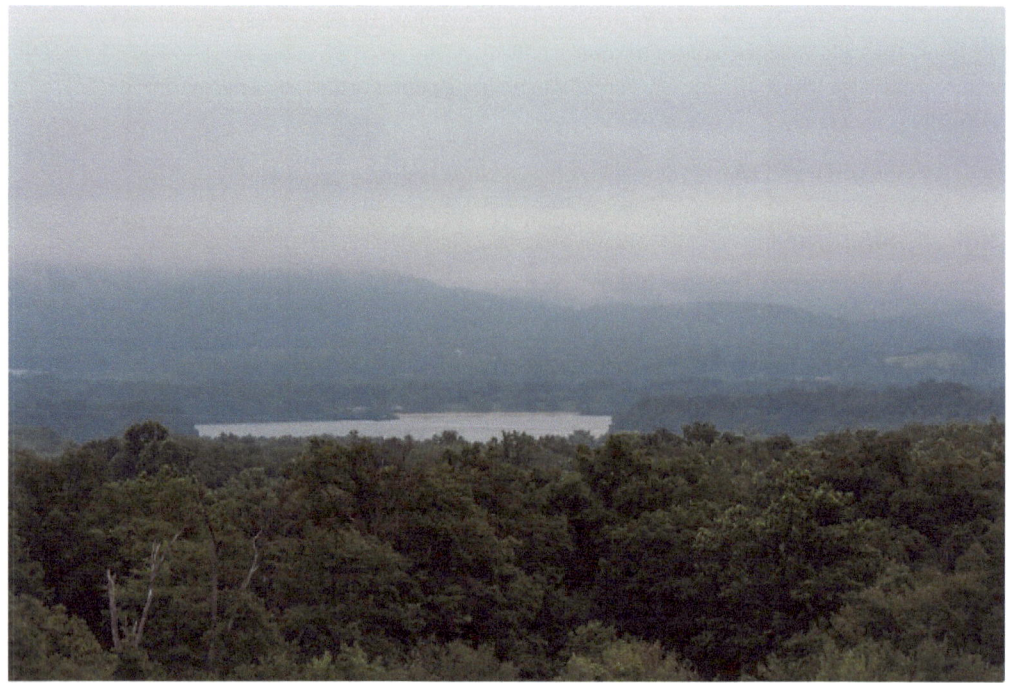

Post production is an important stage for any professional and this is also the case with photographers. Most photographers are aware of the options and facilities that are available in common post production software tools, such as Adobe Photo Essentials. But expert photographers go beyond the Photoshop tool because it cannot simply be used for processing raw images in the best manner. They need software such as Adobe Lightroom. This software comes in the Creative Cloud package of Adobe which is a must for advanced photographers. Here, we discuss some important post production tools and methods that are only used by advanced photographers.

Using Adobe Lightroom CC

Expert photographers cannot rely on the finished composition of the shot by the software present in their DSLR camera. All top photographers work on their photos and then produce a final version using post production techniques. Adobe Lightroom is a powerful software application used by the experts all over the world.

Lightroom has the ability to provide you complete control over the processing of your RAW images. This software application provides access to the Adobe Stock which is used by professional photographers to sell their photos directly to business consumers. You need to access this advanced selling method as well if you would love to compete with the other professionals around the world.

There are powerful elements in this software which are employed by photographers in post production. We earlier discussed the problem of artificial horizon lines created due to camera tilt. The software has the perfect options to change the perspective in order to reduce and in most cases eliminate the distortion that appears in the captured image.

In short, you should eliminate the imaginary horizon and replace it with the real one by carefully tilting the image in post production. The Guided Upright feature in Adobe Lightroom is perfect for this application.

This software should also be used to ensure that you produce the best panoramic photos. It eliminates the needs of cropping because you can improve the boundary lines in the accumulated images and preserve your subject in a better position. This means that your finished panoramic image feels more original and transparent at its end points.

You need to learn that changing the color or brightness in the photo can have multiple effects. Always make a singular change when using image processing software such as Lightroom. Changing the hue, for example should be performed as a single step in order to view and understand its function on the photo.

There are already presents that are available for use in cameras available on smart devices. You can, in fact, design these presets in this excellent software by having complete access to the RGB color channels. You need to understand that daylight shooting often requires a reduction on the blue side of the color spectrum while the photos at the night time need to be moved away from the red end of the spectrum.

This knowledge should be used to create presets that can significantly improve your photography through the use of Adobe applications on smart devices such as Android based phones.

Using PhaseOne Capture One

Capture One was a software tool that was originally developed for specific medium format cameras, but it now works as an independent powerhouse which can give competition to Adobe Lightroom. There are many expert photography techniques that can be better employed in this software. One of the advantages that you can gain using this software is that it is not mainstream. Your finished photo using Capture One will certainly stand out from the rest.

It has a powerful algorithm for finishing RAW images into detailed and very sharp JPEGs. If you especially like to take photos in a noisy environment, then you should switch to this software tool. You need to use the filters and color modification tools available here in order to end up with sharper images with less noise.

The best way to employ this application here is to use its layer based tools. These tools allow you to work on local elements in a picture. Your original version of the photo remains available as long as you have not saved the changes in terms of creating the final TIFF or JPEG file. You can also work on external editors which are allowed on this platform.

Using ON1 Photo 10

Not all photographers can afford the professional Adobe Cloud Service Package. If you are starting professional photography and are short on resources, then you can use this powerful Photo 10 software for editing your photos as an expert. There are effective presets that allow you to improve your RAW images, by changing the settings that cater to photos shot in particular environments such as in low light conditions.

It offers a better learning curve so that you can use just a single software application to start as a novice and end up being an expert post producer in a few weeks. You need to employ the various filters available in ON1 Photo 10 to finally create the best image out of your RAW image data. It can in fact be more powerful than Lightroom, but beaten by the sheer complexity of the complete Adobe Cloud Service package with a flurry of tools.

About the Author

Ryan Crane learned about photography by performing extensive research and then applying the learned principles in the field over a number of years. He is now a well renowned photographer and wants to help others become better at photography as well. He believes that you can become a better photographer, if you can work on your skills and follow the best advices that are on offer in the digital world.

One of the best sources in this regards is the http://improveyourphotographyonline.com/ website which allows you to learn through tutorials and different sessions.

Ryan tries to help inspiring photographers by providing them with a number of image resources such as backgrounds and tutorials. His work is available at http://www.ryancranephotography.com/ and can be viewed by any budding photographer.

www.ingramcontent.com/pod-product-compliance
Lightning Source LLC
Chambersburg PA
CBHW040820200526
45159CB00024B/3067